GOD:
Your Portion

Devotional Christian prayer poems
to unravel the yearnings and mysteries
of your heart, during uncertain times

Author, Designer and Editor
Madhu Kiran Kans

AuthorHouse™ UK
1663 Liberty Drive
Bloomington, IN 47403 USA
www.authorhouse.co.uk
UK TFN: 0800 0148641 (Toll Free inside the UK)
UK Local: 02036 956322 (+44 20 3695 6322 from outside the UK)

Because of the dynamic nature of the Internet, any web addresses or links contained in this book may have changed since publication and may no longer be valid. The views expressed in this work are solely those of the author and do not necessarily reflect the views of the publisher, and the publisher hereby disclaims any responsibility for them.

This book is printed on acid-free paper.

ISBN: 978-1-7283-5640-2 (sc)
ISBN: 978-1-7283-5639-6 (e)

Print information available on the last page.

Published by AuthorHouse 30/12/2022

authorHOUSE®

Dedications

I would like to dedicate this book to everyone around the world, who has lost a loved one to this terrible pandemic.

We all wish we could have spent more time with those we knew but who did not know us so well.

Thank you to my mother Daya Kans for being such an inspiration and for being so patient.

Acknowledgements

I would like to say a big thank you to all the good advice that I have received from Sue Sundstrom, the Institute of Wellbeing, and Vishal Morjaria. As well as all my friends and family who have encouraged me, uplifted me and inspired me on my literary journey. It has been an opportunity to be creative and a privilege to bring the light of Jesus's healing stripes into my readers hearts. Thank you.

A Summertime Of Tenderness

The Summer is here at last
A time of refreshment
A prayerful time of contentment
Where we surrender to the divine echo
And embrace the peace within
Sweet scented aromas
Daffodils and roses
The scent of forgiveness
A virtue of sharing
And belonging to a higher dimension
A Summer full of footsteps and
Dreams and desires
A tender loving lilting
Towards our glory
As we lean upon the majesty of our Nature's Lord
A Summer full of fun
A Summer full of laughter and delight
Yes, a Summer to remember, the whispers of a windswept horizon
Brimming with blessings and holy expectations

A Prayer Poem For Women

Wholesome pureness comes in all sorts of shapes and sizes
By stripping back and seeing the real self
For whom the selfhood really is
And distinguishing it from the ego
A sort of self examination occurs naturally
Automatic, honest appraisal
These heavenly realms within our hearts
This divine wanderlust and curiosity
Identifying and sharpening our dreams
But dreaming without an end in mind
Delving into unknown hurts and limitations
Brings up blockages and lies of the enemy
Lord give us new insights into our
Psychological make up
Into the essence of our truest selves
We can empower and we can grow together
We can have like minded communities
We are all very unique and gifted
We have the power to mould our inner lives, our meditations
Our intuitive giftedness

And we can enrich the world around us and make
a real difference to vulnerable peoples
When our decisions are all ours
When destiny and synchronicity collide
The doors of our inheritance are flung open
The magnificence of our poetry becomes clear
We resonate in this natural healing
We pray with vigour and passion
When we think for ourselves
We cherish each other
Lord thank you for creating us and nurturing us
These lessons become crystal clear
By glorifying the Son, we glorify you
Help us to pray according to your grace
We are being
Transformed from glory to glory
From victory to victory
Our mental health is being enhanced
As we deal with challenging times
And wisdom becomes our best friend
As we leap and take steps of righteousness
We shine our lights into the bleak darkness
We bring fun and laughter into everyone's lives
Harmony and peace fill our footsteps each day
As we praise your Holy name

All For Your Glory

This my GOD manifests
I know that you think he is not cool
In your eyes
But you do not know what I know
Or who He is...
Open your eyes to the truth
Open your eyes to REFLECTION
I am using simple language here
Everything my God manifests
All for His glory
Even the Illuminati
Even the 13 bloodlines
LEELA is His dance in all spheres
Do not hold on to yesterday's grudges
Go and live for today
Be the alive one
THE greatest witness
SEXUALITY belongs to HIM
And it is your greatest gift
As angels chase my shadow
And sing of His glory

All this my GOD MANIFESTS
I can be sensual
I can be erotic
I am all curves
And all self respect!
As He lives in my voice
And in my dance moves
He is never ending and
He winks from time to time
To show me His love and validation
I put on one hat and then I put on another
With so many choices it's mind blowing
So many options
Because of HIS blood
Every knee
Every tongue
Will confess His grace
As all this my God manifests.
All for His Glory

Blessed Intelligence

I am blessed when I realise that
My enemies are worthless and useless
The enemy of man is held captive
All degrading talk is silenced
All lies exposed
And super intelligence rules
This intelligence uplifts
This super intelligence is Holy
This intelligence is independent
And forgiving
And always brings peace
And love to the world
Forever and ever
This intelligence is original
And perpetual
Forever and ever
This is the truth, the life, and the way.

British Sin

GOD forgive us for British Sin
The Sins of the British Military
The whore brothels and exploitation
The campaigns in South Africa
During the Boer War
And the millions who suffered during India's partition
We lift up the Sin of cover ups
We lift up the sins of the Empire days
Yes, there were some good outcomes but also a lot of
Unexplained policies
The subjugation of the native peoples
O so much sin Lord
Splitting up families in immigration detention centres
Taking children from their parents
Forgive us for the 1 million Indian indentured labourers sent
To the colonies where thousands committed suicide
Forgive us for the compensation of £16 billion to slave owners in today's money
Divide and rule
The transatlantic slave trade which affected over 2 million African peoples
The Iraq War where no weapons of mass destruction were found
Thank you for the abolitionists
Forgive us for not knowing our real history
And the history of mankind
All nations have so much sin
All families have so much sin
We lay down this sin at your Cross today
And we bind any future sin to the Cross forever

Lord forgive us for the lies we have believed without question
Forgive us for being so easily manipulated by the media
Forgive the politicians for their near sightedness
Forgive the British Government for creating a hostile environment
Lord forgive us all
Heal us all
You alone know the truth
You alone manifest abundance
Forgive us for our poverty mind sets
Forgive us we pray
Forgive us for cutting corners
Forgive us for not holding people accountable
Forgive us for always taking the easy road
And forgive us for our arrogance
O Lord your love covers all our sins
Your sacrifice covers our shame
How we let down the Jewish people
In Israel, during our time
Lord what have we become?
We don't even recognise ourselves
Open our hearts Lord to confessions
Thank you for your patience

Christian Hope

Thou art greater than depressive thoughts we know
And yet so many suffer quietly and in shame
Breathe through my breath
Linger in my memories
Even black sheep will shine
YOU have poured out your anointment my Lord
You have embellished my life with hope and grace
A deep Christian forgiveness
An overview of dignity
Lord you are the one for me
No other will do, no substitute
No idol can take your place
As I breathe, you empower
You overlook my weaknesses
You enliven with grace, peace and joy
Even these depressive thoughts hint at a new glory
There is a new silver lining emerging
The Holy Spirit descends and anoints forever
O glory to the holy of holies
This is Christian living
This is Christian tolerance
And this is beauty bewildering
Forever and ever,
Full to the brim
Overflowing with pulsating knowledge

Perfection of consciousness
Delirious and happy with your love
This mystery unravels
All I want is to swim inside God
Inside the elixir of life
The elixir of loving creation
Fuller and fuller I become
As my journey into salvation carries me
Upstream and into the fountain
I am delirious again
Full and brimming with life and activity
Life and imagination
The worldly spotlight focuses on my fears
But the sun is bright
And leads to the arts of living
Dramatically, whole-heartedly
Willingly, as life pours forth
Prophesying, pouring forth
Perfecting intimacies
As the world receives the very best of me
Delirious with anticipation
For the betterment of the world

Dear George Floyd

This tragedy was unnecessary
You suffered for all your brothers
The Police officers in Minneapolis have been exposed
Yes, 8 minutes and 46 seconds for your oblivion
According to the British press
Dehumanisation atmosphere still here
Dehumanisation mindset still alive
But my brother at age 46 died
I said my brother at age 46 died
When time stood still and aghast
As spectators watched and gasped
But Derek Chauvin
Robbed you of your dignity, and of your life
Today we shine a light on this madness
O George you will always be remembered
You will always be in our hearts
We will not let your death be in vain
Black lives matter and all minority lives matter
We will not let you be forgotten
During the Coronavirus crisis, your death shook America and the world
Mama, mama! you cried
But the weight of his knee on your neck was too much
You were a black man, a big man, a mighty man
Someone's friend, someone's son, someone's father
Mama, mama! you cried, but no one intervened
Even if you were a petty criminal
How can this be justified, how can this be overlooked?
O George your memory will be kept alive: this tragedy was unnecessary
We vow to keep the memory of your life alive, forever

Fountain Of Life

Full to the brim
Overflowing with pulsating knowledge
Perfection of consciousness
Delirious and happy with your love
This mystery unravels
All I want is to swim inside God
Inside the elixir of life
The elixir of loving creation
Fuller and fuller I become
As my journey into Salvation carries me
Upstream and into the fountain
I am delirious again
Full and brimming with life and activity
Life and imagination
The worldly spotlight focuses on my fears
But the sun is bright
And leads to the arts of living
Dramatically, whole-heartedly
Willingly, as life pours forth
Prophesying, pouring forth
Perfecting intimacies
As the world receives the very best of me
Delirious with anticipation
For the betterment of the world

Full To The Brim

Overflowing with pulsating knowledge
Perfection of consciousness
Delirious and happy with your love
This mystery unravels
All I want is to swim inside God
Inside the elixir of life
The elixir of loving creation
Fuller and fuller I become
As my journey into salvation carries me
Upstream and into the fountain
I am delirious again
Full and brimming with life and activity
Life and imagination
The worldly spotlight focuses on my fears
But the sun is bright
And leads to the arts of living
Dramatically, whole-heartedly
Willingly, as life pours forth
Prophesying, pouring forth
Perfecting intimacies
As the world receives the very best of me
Delirious with anticipation
For the betterment of the world

Grace

Lord all we need is sexual healing
And the grace and graciousness of your Son
The mercy of validation of being
True birthing, true salvation
Holy, holy, holy is the Lord God almighty
Who was, and is, and is to come
Holy, holy, holy is the nectar of healing
For your words are well chosen
And our pain at times seems supreme
However your living Word will uplift
Your living light will find soft hearts
The Saints bow down to bless
This inner beauty which has been tainted
Yet with stimulating sounds this healing continues
Your garden of mystery evolves
Here is the perfect decision
Here is the perfect forgiveness
We forgive ourselves for being too vulnerable
We forgive our tenderness and naivety
We need all types of healing
And out of nowhere comes a divine appointment
A desire to be whole again
Random events collide with spontaneous movements
In tune with each other
In tune with life itself

For we will give love and receive love gently
As we heal and communicate
As we are empowered out of silence
We bow down to your wonder
We bow down to your power to heal
And let go this vast trauma
A trauma of childhood injustice
A trauma that is so vivid
A black scar of scapegoat energy
A new life will begin
A new way of seeing the world
But this healing takes time
This healing comes with tears
A final surrender of our psyches
A final acknowledgement of all lies
Our enemy is defeated
Our purpose is solidified
Holy, holy, holy is the Lord God almighty
Amen

Healing

Lord God all I need is a divine healing
A validation of being
I desire true birthing, true freedom, true salvation
Where even the saints bow to bless me
Where my inner beauty is everlasting
As I stimulate your heart and mind
As I make you think
With this unique power
Which surpasses all imagination
A guided creativity
A garden of mysteries
Yes, I am alive due to a unique calling
Yes, I am created divine, due to a unique decision
The Lord my God is brilliant
The Lord my God is sublime
The Lord my God is spontaneous
The Lord my God is available
Yet I am not my thoughts
I am not my body, I am my heart and my breath
I long to give and receive love
Flourishing with every heartbeat
The Lord my God is full of grace

The Lord my God is full of love
It's the Lord's healing I seek
It's the Lords healing I deserve
This unfoldment is quite unique
This wonder in the air
The divinity of kindness
And sharing
An explosion of dreaming
A memory of sweetness
Give us refinement Lord
Give us happiness and joy
Lord God's divine life giving grace
Lord God's healthy questioning mind
Thank you for this healing time
Thank you for your ascended masters
Thank you for all our sufferings and heartbreaks
We centre our souls on you
We meditate on your supreme Love always

Honey

Sweet Honey, you are the ultimate child of God
A creation of the potters kiln
A glory unlike any other
God shines His face upon you today
You have been oppressed
You sweet Honey who has been usurped
You are so pure and innocent
You are so holy and sacred

The King himself anoints you today
The King invites you to his Kingdom
And esteems you and your talents
You are pure
You are clean
You are fresh
And sweet Honey your time has come
To shine like no other
To sing like no other
To dance like no other soul
For you are His anointed
You sweet Honey are a child of God

How Blessed Am I

Lord how blessed am I, the daughter of supreme divinity
Lord how blessed am I, the child of the holy King
Lord how blessed am I, a woman of many talents

Opening myself up to all your glory and healing
My story will inspire millions
To be more compassionate
To be more active
To be more assertive and genuine

O Lord thank you for this unique framework
Thank you for my gracious healing journey
Lord how blessed am I
All things will work together
All for your glory

Lord Thank you for all your blessings in my life
Lord how blessed am I
IN THE FLOW
I am in the flow now
Anointed and appointed by grace
I am only human though
Sometimes even I can dwell on all
The bad things that have happened
In my life, but we are all called to move on

And not hold grudges
To forgive 77 times
As Royal Priestesses
With diamond tunes of fire
We are the blessed amongst the blessed
Pure and superb
Holy and full of self esteem
We are in the flow always
And we breathe the flow of life forever
Just by sighing we can bring positivity into this dark world
Just by being we can bring joy to so many people
This water of wisdom flows through us
And is sprinkled over us every day and in every moment

Amen

In The Name Of Jesus

In His name I cast off all feelings of low self-esteem
In His name I cast out all the lies of the enemy
In His name I cast off all laziness and poor decision making

In His name I pray for self actualisation
In His name I pray for a time for meditation
In His name I pray for heaven's delight
In His name I pray for financial freedom
In His name I pray for blessings upon blessings

In His name I cast off self doubt
In His name I cast out the burdens of illness
In His name I cast out the desire for more and more stuff
In His name I cast out the belief that I am not good enough

In His name I pray for fulfilment
In his name I pray for romance and cherished times
In His name I pray for love and forgiveness
In His name I pray for a burning need to make a difference
In His name I pray for happiness and contentment

Amen

Interfaith

Interconnections of inclusion
International allusions
The growth of inter-culture
Faith in differences
Respect for diversity
Interconnected religions
Jesus of Nazareth
Our ultimate transcender of reality
Faith across ages
Faith across races
Faith flowering spontaneously
Interconnections of soulfulness
The divine volumes of scripture
Noble wisdom and kind acceptance
Through the act of love and forgiveness
Interfaith Faith
Blessings of genuine sincere grace
Introspection and contemplation
The world of inner faith
Enhanced by society
Enhanced by community
Inside accumulations
Of the wealth of peace
Interesting power, interesting choice
The path of pureness
The path of interfaith

It's My Time

This sex is not for sale
This sex is for creating
Cavorting and enjoying
My sexuality is my delicacy
No shame is this activity
No shame of my erogenous zones
Touch me here, touch me there
This sexiness oozes all over
Immersed in sensuality
Erotic expectations and full blown natural joyfulness
It's my decision, it's my body
The glory of my sex
Yes I want to enjoy the glory of my sex
Thank you Lord Jesus for this glory
This ultimate persuasion
An expression of uniqueness
The glory of my virgin light
A propensity to be fully in the moment
A desire to fully expel my liquids
A wonder at my own satisfaction
These wonderful highlights of erotica
And foreplay
A playful tenderness gives way
This is the glory of my sexiness
In a wonderful marriage

Jesus The Living Stone

JESUS you are my rock and you are my living stone
The most powerful of God's holy trinity
Jesus you are the living joy
The heart of my heart
The redeemer from Heaven
The giver of life
Jesus you are the holy charm
The divine music and pure delight of my heart
Jesus you are the living rock and the living stone
Who transforms and blesses
Who brings grace to life's tradgedies
You are the healing balm who brings hope to millions
And grace to all who really listen
Lord JESUS you are the great intercessor
The lovely light of lights and the greatest gift to mankind

Limitations Of The Mind

Our limitations define us
But our overcoming these limitations inspires us
For we have been blessed with an abundance of creativity
An abundance of imagination
And an abundance of forgiveness

Our uniqueness is the beginning of hope
Our uniqueness is the ability to choose
We can grow and ponder
We can aspire and breathe
We can commune with the sacred life force

We are all yearning for fulfilment
We are all yearning for acceptance
Our holy imaginations set us on fire
We need to nurture our inner lives

We need to browse the spiritual hinterland
And let this inner voice reap victory
O Lord help us to possess our limitations
Help us to let go and rise into our greatness

Living By Faith

This is Living by faith
Living without any restraints
In a positive and risk-taking way
Lively and adventurous
Holy and sacred
Living as if there is no tomorrow
Full of fun and full of joy
Let the unexpectedness of life stream through
And fill us with inspiration
And bewilderment always
The flow of the Holy waters
The rivers of healing
A new found confidence
And a wonderful persuasion
The life worth living
A life worthy of the women of God

Logical Conclusions

In order to live there must be death
In order to laugh there are many tears
To give meaning to life we need to let go of life
Sometimes facing up to reality and the truths of Salvation
The truth about our mortality
The truth about the lies we tell
The truth about our limitations
And unexpected growth
A path out of our comfort zone
Enables us to really shine
And can lead to many gifts
If we can accept new offerings
Offerings of delight
What might seem like obstacles can lead to resolutions
What might seem like fantasies leads to our enhancements
We can glory in our insights and glory in our weaknesses
But Lord God knows our frustrations and disappointments
All power and grace to Him

My Spiritual Sexiness

A soft-bodied exquisiteness
Daring to believe in the unbroken-self
Chance meetings which seem to be enhancing and
Divine appointments which are enabling

My spiritual sexiness can enlighten
Even my enemies, even my intellect
For this is the heart of who I am
The heart of my presence
The world needs to know how sexy I really am
And how sweet and honest

I declare a synchronicity of healings
I declare a beauty within
I declare multi – orgasmic manifestations
I declare a divine sensuality
This is the new HEAVEN
AND this is the new EARTH
My spiritual sexiness has been awakened
Wholesome pureness comes in all sorts of sizes
Stripping back the lies of the Universal Mind
The satans of this material world
Here deep inside a real calm
A confidence beyond boundaries
AS we resonate in the trueness of our sex
Yes divine is this gift and wonderful the enjoyment
The lips quiver in anticipation
My heart beats in rhythmic beats
My divine sexiness illumines my being
And breathes new life into my identity

'My Portion, My Deliverance

O Saviour of man
Living Word,
Holy love of loves
Thank you for reminding me of me of my untold sins

Let me remember and cry
As I am tempted
As I was usurped
For you are my portion, my deliverance

Give me my judgement daily
With your kind wisdom
And your divinity
I say again, You are my portion
You are my deliverance
And You are my love

I am no longer deprived or depraved
By your grace
I am no longer a sinner amongst sinners
Wipe away my sinful memories
Restore my heart to its innocent perceptions
Infuse me with the pureness and the purity of creation
For you are my portion, my deliverance
As I long to see you face to face

And your kindness overwhelms me
I tremble, I hear, I see
This goodness is real
This goodness is free, and gives life everlasting

O King
O Holy Sanctifier
Justify my true-self
Let me repent again
Forgive me Lord and make me worthy
Of your light
Of your portion
Of your deliverance

Praises to the Lord
Praises to the God of Creation
Obedience to Him
Wrap me up in your aroma
The fragrance of Heaven
And a beauty bewildering
For you are my portion, my deliverance
Only you can wipe away my tears
Only You can enliven me with Hope

And make me holy
Refine my mind
Praises to the Lord
Praises to the God of Creation
Obedience to Him
Wrap me up in your aroma
The fragrance of Heaven

And a beauty bewildering
For you are my portion, my deliverance
Only you can wipe away my tears
And make me holy and worthy of your love
Refine my mind
As my thoughts are unrelenting
A mind full of desires
I surrender
My self doubt to Your Majesty

Select a new Song, O Heavenly Father
Nurture this special child
During this special time
A time of growth
A time of assurance
That Providence is the will of the Lord God
Abundance fills the air
For you are my portion, my deliverance
And I praise your holy name Christ Jesus, Christ Jesus

Thank you for listening
And interceding
Thank you giving and receiving
My heart, my body, my soul, my imagination
For you are my portion, and my deliverance
Forever, and ever Amen

My Rose Of Life

As I smell the aroma of life
I am drawn to a fantasy time
As I touch the petals of life
I am pricked by life's lessons
As I water the plants of life
I am nurturing my very own soul
As I gaze at the colours of life
I am at awe, now and forever more
As I offer you the colours of life
I am blessed with the wealth of compassion
As I show you how to care for the buds of life
I am entirely cared for
As I water the leaves of life
I am cleansed and naturally baptised

Peace

The deaths of our old selves may seem scary
Our longings and yearnings hint at changes we need to make
To a new way of seeing and being
But it is the deaths of our too serious selves that will enhance us
A little laughter goes a long way
Even our tears can be meaningful
Our tears can heal us, so let go of all our pain
In order to appreciate fully we need some disappointments
And face up to our shortcomings
Our limitations and weaknesses
We need to be honest with ourselves
The path out of our comfort zones
Leads to higher learning
And intensified growth
If only we can accept these new offerings
Offerings of grace
Offerings of delights
Our hindrances will lead to our growth
Rest in this new glory of creating your own path
Rest in this new understanding
Rest in the holy light of God
And these holy synchronicities of pure joy

Quaerere Verum

Here it comes! THE next installment correlating everything and affecting Life
The Kingdom of God is expanding whether you can see or not
Laugh out loud all the people of all the nations
Almighty God is breathing forever
Laugh out loud people of good conversation
Wink and smile angels of light
Our Guardians are always on our side
Communicating through the Eucharist
The blood and the flesh
Let us drink the blood and eat the flesh
Yes this is the instalment
It overflows and uplifts
Mankind from misery
The living Son and of all his grace
Fully perfect
Fully infinite
In pursuit of all of us
Me and you
Glory of glories
Song of Songs

The party of Heaven
The holiest Yahweh
This life of sweetness
And inspiration
Shines into our midst
When we surrender and forgive
But forgiving can be very difficult
It takes courage and patience
Help us to grow according to your wisdom
To use the inner ear to seek the Holy Spirit
In the silence is where we meet our creator
This is where everything comes to life
Quaerere Verum
My God is alive
My God has perfect authority
I allow Him to lead and purify
I allow Him to show me the way forward
To the next decision
To God's abundance and sacredness
Amen, Amen

Restoration

O Lord help us to understand your amazing kindness
You have given us your holy grace and sacrificial love
Let us understand how much we owe to you
Lord God we are ready for your incredible restoration
We long for more and more communication
You alone we revere
You alone we praise
Holy, holy, holy
Your loving arms embrace us
Kindness is the keystone for everlasting communion with your love
In you we seek and find our inner charms
Our inner yearnings
Our sensitive delights
Only in you do we have all our needs met
Restoration for the nation
Restoration for our families
Heal, all our wounds known and unknown
So that we can be salt and light to the dark realms around us
So that we can truly heal and be there for each other
Expel our deep anxieties
Empower us forever
Lord your graciousness bewilders us
You Jesus you are the King of our lives

Sculpture

There is exquisiteness in your breath
I see the exquisiteness of your smile
Your whole outline is unique
The sculpture of your serenity is complete

As I look into your eyes, I see oceans of love
As I brush your hair, there are beautiful doves above
Your white and silver robes dazzle my eyes
In your palms I see pilgrim's eyes

You are all perfect and all modesty
Your elegance is noble
Your heart is larger than life
For the sculpture of your serenity is complete

The smoothness of your skin
The fashion that you choose
All the colours of summer
A rainbow of truth for you

Starting Again

As I start again,, with this life of moving, being unsettled
Always searching for something new
Seeking a new environment
A new area of specialism, a new area of study
A new type of education
For the new woman I am becoming
What patterns can I change
What new insights can I discover
What is really happening and how can I move forward with my dreams
However the demonic barriers continue to rear their heads
A feeling of unworthiness
A deep desire to escape
Unrelenting resentment and disgrace
What have I become, whom am I trying to delude
This helplessness is intertwined with loathing
An inner turmoil
Open to interpretation
I long for a new life
A being and wholeness that I have yet to experience

I need this
I need to trust again
Otherwise I am starting again
Beginning from a hurt that has overtaken my sanity
My mental health is peeling and collapsing
Nothing makes sense, there is death all round
All I see is distancing
Social distancing and unusual masks
As the fabric of our society fades away
I no longer socialise frequently
I am stuck in this morbid time
Of Covid - 19 death announcements
O Lord have mercy
STOP THIS MADNESS
Let me be frivolous again
Let me travel and explore again and have a little fun again
And then the knee went down on George Floyd's neck and the shudder
Of looking at how terrible humans can be went up my fragile spine

'Mama Mama' I heard him cry
8minutes and 46 seconds later
According to the British Press
Another death statistic
But one witnessed over social media
' Mama, mama:'
' I just killed a black man'
But no remorse, no tears from the police officer
So here I start again, remembering the times that I too have been harassed
I have to believe that something positive will come from this level of pain and anger
I stand alone at this turning point, as we all do
Is this really happening?
My friend
I stand and I cry
I kneel and I empathise
So many institutions need to change
Get rid of this dehumanisation
And let me smell joy
Let me believe in mankind again
And let me laugh at least once again

Sweet Silence

The realms of silence deep within
Infinity growing and expanding
The pregnant moment of life
This sweet silence entices us
Out of sweetness comes the word
Out of silence the echo
Calm, pure, stable and profound
Endearing and demure
Golden silence where life begins
Peaceful silence
Encouraging silence
The new philosophy of light

Peace, truth, love and bliss
In the depth of my mind and heart
I touch everyday with silence
In total surrender to art
Time passes, time ticks
Yet all is timeless
Silence remains silent
Fathomless, wide, and contrary
The sweetest silence of dreams
A breath-taking uniqueness of life
A breath-taking uniqueness of paradise

The Blessings Of The Firstborn

The blessings of the firstborn
Will be bestowed on the firstborns of all nations and tribes
Male and female, great and small
For all Holy and sacred children of God
With pure and innocent hearts
Blessed are those that bless them and cursed are those that
Curse them...
I claim the mighty blessings of the first born
I claim the blessings of all good kingdoms
I claim all my tears of disappointment
For blessed are those who mourn
And blessed are the pure in heart
Blessed are the innocents
Who have been forcefully and psychologically abused
Blessed are the poor for they shall see God's face
And they will inherit Heaven and Earth
Yes blessed are all firstborns of all nationalities
Yes Lord JESUS blessed are the firstborn
Who emerge from the dew of Heaven.
However the Kingdom of God is always forcefully expanding

The Lord's Last Supper

I am sharing the Lord's last supper
I eat the bread with Him
I drink the wine with Him
This is a time for my destiny
Where everything is being created and re-created
The Lord's supper is real
The Lord's supper is mighty
An inclusion to angels and their wealth of love and protection
An invitation to hear with the inner ear
A calling out of the wilderness and into the festivities
A transformation from the blackest of sheeps to a white angel of glory
As I share the Lord''s supper I know that you see the real me
I have the King by my side, the King by my soul
As I share the Last supper
And in HIS words of wisdom
I am blessing those who bless me
And forgiving those who need to be forgiven

The Father Wound, The Mother Wound

These are the wounds of divine pre destiny
All rejection, all mental health challenges
A wounding that may appear as if it came from nowhere
To an innocent and helpless child
The father wound may be camouflaged for a while
The mother wound may slowly fade away
O Lord God thank for these wounds and afflictions
As they are limited and can be reframed
These wounds have their back stories, these wounds were so unpredictable
O earthly papa, you did not know how your mind
raced with negativity and depression
And this led to paranoid schizophrenia and a shattering of your soul
As your ambitions were thwarted by factory vouchers
This institutionalisation was a nightmare for you and for us
Finally we forgave and moved on
And the Lord shows us His purposes
These thorns will finally fall out
And give way to the sweet scent of an abundant Life
However it is these wounds that make us
They supply character and resilience
And help us to ponder on the wounds of our Lord
On the cross at Calvary
Ponder on this special sacrificial blood
The blood shed for a New Covenant
A new vibration and a new way of being
Where Your Gospel comes alive
By Your grace and for Your glory
Amen

The Thorns In My Heart

Lord these thorns in my heart
Remind me of your holy suffering
And these thorns in my flesh
Of your wonderful salvation
Pierce me and pierce my being
Let me cry recklessly
Help me to pour out my anguish
Let these thorns of regret not affect me
Help me to forgive myself
Help me Lord to forget all transgressions
Lord Jesus I claim your benevolence
I claim your innocence
O Lord allow this healing to continue
Piercing my flesh and my body
Piercing my heart too
As I cry and experience the loneliest parts of myself
O Lord your blood covers all my wounds
Transform me and transform my life
Help me to surrender and let go
Help me to move forward and rise above these inner storms
Your Word embedded in my soul
The words of life
The words of love
The words of self discovery

O Lord in you alone I seek my Salvation
But most of all I seek your protection
And your guidance
As I am dealing with many disappointments
Help me Lord to be honest with myself
Let my life journey be a special flowering
A space for reflection
And contemplation
But most importantly let me be surrounded by your Holy Spirit
Touched by your lovely peaceful embrace
And the prayers of your Son
As I sing to you my King
These thorns turn to rosebuds
This testing turns into blessings of victory
Thank you for the thorns in my side and the
Thorns in my beautiful heart

The Visions Of Holy Intelligence

During these visions of our intellects
Comes a birthing of superb consciousness
There is a supremacy of artistic culture
And a defining moment in our history
The beauty of inner sanctuary
An inner sanctum of feminine wisdom
A wonderful peaceful purity
As I explore divine and stupendous sexuality
Begin by asking the right questions of our leaders
During social distancing world wide
A barrage of reporting deaths across nations
This conspiracy with our hearts and minds
A play on our anxieties
With the mainstream media under their control
O Illuminati
You have culminated in a new dearth of investigations
There is a liberal world view at stake
Holy visions of dignified intelligences
Women of the world arise
Into your destiny of new empowerment
Take a hold of this new life
With new extreme challenges
And bless the whole world with your visionary wisdom
And an inner ultimate beauty

O women
Of integrity
Superbly anointed in the stillness of your architecture
Looking inwards towards our philosophy
Arise and be outspoken
Arise and feel fulfilled
Taking risks that we never imagined
Leading by example
Arise and shout for joy
The joy of the Lord
For these visions of our sublime intellects
Forge a new border
Bring down strongholds within our families
And are filled with a rugged perception and
An inner knowing
An inner calculation
Perfect and pure peace
Visions of great sensitivity
The breath of honey supreme

The Voice Of Modern Democracy

Ain't nobody gonna stop me now
Ain't nobody gonna manipulate me
No neo Nazis here
No bullying the sacred
No liars here
Ain't no room for extremism
Ain't no one left sane in the Cabinet
The pen will still beat the sword
This word of truth will endure
No matter what the cost
No matter what your rage
No neo Nazis here
This rapid deterioration of my civil rights
This grand puzzle
A muzzle of free minds
Call it what you will
Fascism is living in our back garden
We have allowed it to grow
Through some kind of complacency
Some kind of hijacking
But ain't nobody going to muzzle my voice
The true voice of democracy

This divine voice
Rise and rise my self esteem
To know the very best of me
Rise and rise the voices of dissent
Rise and rise the living testament
Ain't nobody going to mess with my voice
Ain't nobody going to mess with the voice of modern democracy
Shout for all truth
Speak up for vulnerable peoples
Ain't no one going to mess with the voice of reason
The voice of life
This voice of pragmatism
The voice of shining liberty

This Is My Land, This Is My Home

This land belongs to me
All the trees in this land belong to me
All the lakes belong to me
The wheat, the barley, and all the honey
All the milk belongs to me
The stars in the sky belong to me
Even the sun belongs to me

There is a fire beneath my feet that burns for justice
There is a fire within my bosom that burns for life
Yes this whole land belongs to me
And all the islands in the ocean belong to me
However you have raped this land it will be restored
However you have defiled this soil, it will produce abundance
For this is truly my land
And the land of my forefathers
Therefore it is blessed by the God Almighty

This is the new life of being in the glory of
My God and being in his presence
This is the new grace of everlasting abundance
Where there is no worry
Where there are no dilemma
All things will be found in his glorious riches
All directions will be found in his voice
For my lord Jesus reigns supreme
My lord Jesus encourages fulfilment
This is the new dawning and new simplicity
This is where everything comes alive
Where there is much positive thinking
And genuine contemplation
So much nurturing and hope
This new life is awaiting all his disciples
This new life is permeating all our shortcomings
All for his Glory
All for his Grace
Amen Amen

This My God Manifests

This my God manifests
I know you think he is not cool
In your eyes
But you do not know what I know
Or anything about who he is...
Open your life to the truth
Open your life to reflection
I am using simple language
Everything my God manifests
Even the illuminati
Even the 13 bloodlines
Leela is his dance in all spheres
Do not hold grudges from yesterday
Go and live for today
Be the alive one
The greatest witness
My sexuality belongs to me
Angles chase my shadow
And I sing His Glory
All this my God manifests

I can be sensual
I am all curves
And all self respect
As he lives in my voice
And in my dance moves
He is never ending
He winks now and then to show his love and validation
I put one foot in front of the other
Having so many choices is mind blowing
Having forgiven 77 times, I am moving on from people who need to be forgiven
So many options
So much grace
Every knee will bow
Every tongue will confess
His grace as well as His BLESSINGS
As I glorify my King forever

This Ultimate Reality

The ultimate reality
Lies deep within my breathless heart
Deep within my sorrowful glare
All my memories will fine tune themselves
A luxury of openness
Even when I sleep
This ultimate reality widens as I dream
And a book of sounds comes gushing out
The ocean within me
This restless desire
A longing for union and intimacy
A perpetual call to creation
Ultimate reason, ultimate fascination
I ponder and muse on all that is unsaid
Between the lines
Of the Ten Commandments
Imagine what poetry we can write
With Heaven divine
The touch of angels' wings
Of my subtle and ultimate homecoming
And all the ultimate answers to all my questions
O blessed am I, who is alive and
Life flows on to a spontaneous and refined maturity

For blessed are those who cry in anguish
And blessed are those who mourn
The ultimate reality is forever changing
This ultimate reality is forever deepening
Heard melodies are so sweet but those unheard are sweeter
Soft pipes play on...
But not to the unrefined ear but to the more exquisite
Inner ear, and for my reality
Show me your personification of hope and let my heart burn
With this new reality
Of love, of tenderness, of cherished looks from lovers
Yes this new reality is what I seek
What I always long for
Where time and space stand still
And where suddenly everything makes sense

To Stay Contented, Stay Happy

In this Covid 19 interlude, I look to my Saviour
I revel in His glory, for everything I have belongs to Him
And everything He has created belongs to me
All of creation, all of his loving nature
To stay contented, stay happy and be joyful
During this Covid 19 interlude, everything becomes a Jesus interval
Beauty of the bewilderment of new life
A new holy birth out of a desire to please only Him
Healing baptism, a new found passion
To stay contented, stay happy and be joyful
This dreaming of a new kind of friendship
This inevitable letting go
Surrender, yes I surrender, to your power
Your grace, your super magical light
Whether I am working or not
Whether I am furloughed or not
I stay contented, stay happy and be joyful
Now that the bigger picture appears
I do not need to feel sorry for myself
Do not need to feel angry at my exploiters and enemies
Do not need to remember any betrayals
But I stay contented, stay happy and be joyful

Transformation

Crossing over a delightful chasm
Thereby leading to more and more inspiration
A germination of happiness and tapping into all possibilities
This fulfilment in pleasing God and not people
Reflecting and accommodating life's flow
A better understanding of what it means to be human
A winning combination of heartfelt concerns
This new definition of determination
With a revised rigorous framework
A becoming into being
The being of the everlasting
A graciousness that leads us to see God's goodness
This time of lockdown allows for our evolution
Be still and know that I am God!
Of deeper self reflection, and appreciating the aliveness of everyday life
Seeing with new eyes the subtleties of the natural world
Here at last is Heaven's beauty on Earth
Here is Heaven's grace
It's all in our myriad perceptions
Certain unique points of view
Never look back, just breathe forward
Breath by breath
Beauty upon beauty
Again living in just being, observing and feeling

Women

Wholesome pureness comes in all sorts of shapes and sizes
The beauty of stripping back and seeing the real self
For who the self really is and why it was created...
Women, you are God's holy angles
Natural mothers
Divine protectors
Let us examine our hearts and minds
Identify and sharpen our dreams
We have so much splendour and wisdom within our hearts

So much caring and sharing to do
Let us work together and with unity
Where destiny and unity collide
For we are wholesome and pure forever
At inception
At the beginning of creation
And the magnificence of our poetry becomes clear
The poetry within our hearts and souls
For we are women, created in God's image

Created to nurture, created to listen, created to lead
Almighty God thank you for blessing us
Almighty God thank you for showering us with your Grace
Help us to reflect your true Glory
Help us to be the holy women that you created us to be
Amen

You Are The One

You are the One
The One that God has specifically chosen
And blessed since before the beginning of time
The One who is always nurturing
The One who has put your yesterdays in their place
The One who is spontaneous
The One who gives life
The One who forgives
It is you who are the digital genius
And the High intellectual
You are the One with all God's blessings
With All His glory
And the dew of Heaven
You are the One who has His divine mystery
Forever and ever
God bless you always
Amen

Peace I leave with you; my peace I give to you. I do not
give to you as the world gives. Do not let your hearts
be troubled, and do not be afraid. JOHN 14: 27 (NIV)

Printed in the United States
by Baker & Taylor Publisher Services